The Complete Guide to Risotto

The Complete Guide to Risotto

Delicious Recipes and Expert Techniques

Edwin Beltran

Nuqui Ricardo Regala

CONTENTS

DEDICATION	xi
Preface	1
Prologue	3
1 Introduction to Risotto	5
What is Risotto?	7
History of Risotto	9
The Basics of Risotto Making	11
2 Classic Risotto Recipes	13
Recipe: Mushroom Risotto	16
Recipe: Asparagus Risotto	18
Recipe: Saffron Risotto	20

CONTENTS

Recipe: Tomato Risotto — 22

Recipe: Pumpkin Risotto — 24

3 Seafood Risotto Recipes — 26

Recipe: Shrimp and Pea Risotto — 29

Recipe: Scallop Risotto — 31

Recipe: Lobster Risotto — 33

Recipe: Crab Risotto — 35

4 Meat Risotto Recipes — 37

Recipe: Chicken Risotto — 40

Recipe: Beef Risotto — 42

Recipe: Sausage and Peppers Risotto — 44

Recipe: Pork and Apple Risotto — 46

5 Vegetable Risotto Recipes — 48

Recipe: Spinach and Feta Risotto — 51

Recipe: Butternut Squash and Sage Risotto — 53

CONTENTS

Recipe: Roasted Red Pepper Risotto   55

Recipe: Eggplant and Tomato Risotto   58

6   Risotto Accompaniments   60

Garlic Bread Recipe   62

Mixed Green Salad Recipe   64

Grilled Vegetables Recipe   65

Roasted Chicken Recipe   66

7   Advanced Techniques and Tips   68

Stock Preparation   71

Risotto Variations   73

Cooking for Large Groups   75

Presentation and Plating Tips   77

8   Conclusion   79

9   Bonus Recipes   82

Bonus Recipe 1: Mushroom and Parmesan Risotto   83

CONTENTS

Bonus Recipe 2: Lemon and Shrimp Risotto 85

Bonus Recipe 3: Tomato and Basil Risotto 87

Bonus Recipe 4: Truffle Risotto 89

Creative Recipe 1: Risotto with butternut squash, goat cheese, and crispy sage 91

Creative Recipe 2: Risotto with wild mushrooms, caramelized onions, and a splash of white truffle oil 93

Creative Recipe 3: Risotto with fresh peas, lemon, and mint 96

Creative Recipe 4: Risotto with sausage, kale, and Parmesan cheese 98

Creative Recipe 5: Risotto with lobster, saffron, and brandy 100

Vegan Recipe 1: Vegan risotto with roasted butternut squash, sage, and cashew cream 102

CONTENTS

Vegan Recipe 2: Vegan risotto with roasted beetroot, walnuts, and vegan goat cheese 105

Vegan Recipe 3: Vegan risotto with wild mushrooms, thyme, and cashew cream 108

Vegan Recipe 4: Vegan risotto with roasted Brussels sprouts, garlic, and vegan sausage 111

Epilogue 114

Glossary of Terms 115

ALSO BY THE AUTHOR 117

Copyright © 2023 by Edwin Beltran

All rights reserved. No part of this book may be reproduced in any manner whatsoever without written permission except in the case of brief quotations embodied in critical articles and reviews.

While every precaution has been taken in the production of this book, the publisher assumes no responsibility for errors or omissions, or for damage resulting from the information contained herein.

First Printing, 2023

Cover photo by Wallace Araujo

To Coleen, Sky and Neo. You are my inspirations.

Preface

Risotto is a timeless dish that has been enjoyed by people all around the world for generations. This creamy, comforting dish is a staple in many Italian households, and it has gained a well-deserved reputation as a gourmet meal.

As someone who has always been passionate about cooking and exploring new flavors, I have been enamored with risotto since my first bite. Over the years, I have experimented with countless variations of this classic dish, and I have learned a lot about what makes a good risotto and what can go wrong.

This book is the result of my many years of experience cooking and experimenting with risotto. Whether you're a seasoned home cook or a beginner in the kitchen, this book has something for you. I've included classic risotto recipes as well as more adventurous variations that are sure to impress your guests.

In addition to providing you with delicious recipes, I've also included tips and techniques that will help you perfect your risotto-making skills. From selecting the right rice to achieving the perfect consistency, I'll guide you through every step of the process.

I hope that this book will inspire you to experiment with

new flavors and techniques, and that it will become a trusted resource in your kitchen. So, grab your apron and let's get started!

Prologue

Risotto is one of those dishes that seems intimidating at first, but with a little practice and guidance, it can become a staple in your cooking repertoire. It's a dish that rewards patience and attention to detail, and it's incredibly versatile - you can make it with almost any combination of ingredients.

I still remember the first time I tried risotto. I was at a fancy Italian restaurant, and I had no idea what to expect. But from the first bite, I was hooked. The creamy texture, the complex flavors - it was like nothing I had ever tasted before. I knew that I had to learn how to make it myself.

Over the years, I've made risotto countless times - for family dinners, for dinner parties, and even just for myself on a lazy Sunday afternoon. I've experimented with different ingredients and techniques, and I've learned a lot along the way.

In this book, I want to share everything that I've learned about risotto. I want to demystify this dish and show you that it's not as difficult as it may seem. Whether you're a seasoned home cook or a beginner in the kitchen, I believe that you can make delicious risotto with the right guidance.

So, let's dive in and explore the wonderful world of risotto together. I hope that this book will inspire you to get creative in the kitchen and to discover your own favorite flavor combinations. Enjoy!

1

Introduction to Risotto

Risotto is a classic Italian dish that has been enjoyed for centuries. This creamy, comforting dish is made with arborio rice, which is slowly cooked in a broth until it reaches a creamy, velvety consistency. Risotto can be made with a variety of ingredients, including meat, seafood, vegetables, and herbs, making it a versatile dish that can be adapted to suit any taste.

In this chapter, we'll explore the basics of risotto, including its history and the essential ingredients and techniques needed to make it. Here's what you can expect to learn:

- What is Risotto? We'll start by defining what risotto is and what makes it different from other rice dishes.
- History of Risotto: We'll take a brief look at the history of risotto, tracing its roots back to medieval Italy and exploring how it has evolved over time.

- The Basics of Risotto Making: We'll cover the essential ingredients and techniques needed to make risotto, including selecting the right rice, preparing the broth, and cooking the rice to achieve the perfect texture.

By the end of this chapter, you'll have a solid understanding of what risotto is and what it takes to make it. So, let's get started!

What is Risotto?

Risotto is a classic Italian dish made with arborio rice that is cooked slowly in a broth until it becomes creamy and velvety. The dish is known for its rich, comforting flavor and texture, and it can be made with a variety of ingredients, such as meat, seafood, vegetables, and herbs.

What sets risotto apart from other rice dishes is its cooking method. Unlike other rice dishes where the rice is boiled and drained, risotto is cooked by adding broth to the rice one ladleful at a time and stirring constantly until the liquid is absorbed. This slow and steady process releases the starch from the rice, creating a creamy texture that is characteristic of risotto.

One of the key things that sets risotto apart from other rice dishes is its texture. Because the rice is cooked slowly and the liquid is added in small amounts over time, the starch is released gradually, resulting in a creamy and velvety texture that is not found in other rice dishes. The rice still retains a bit of bite, however, so it's not mushy like some other rice dishes can be.

Another thing that makes risotto unique is its versatility. While the basic recipe involves cooking arborio rice with broth and stirring in butter and Parmesan cheese, you can add a variety of other ingredients to create endless flavor combinations. For example, you could make a mushroom risotto by sautéing mushrooms with garlic and shallots and adding them to the rice, or a seafood risotto by adding shrimp, scallops, or lobster to the mix.

Risotto is also a dish that requires attention and patience. You can't simply set it and forget it like you might with other rice dishes. The constant stirring and adding of broth require your full attention, but the result is well worth the effort. Many people find the process of making risotto to be relaxing and almost meditative.

Risotto can be served as a main course or as a side dish, and it is often paired with wine and a variety of accompaniments, such as garlic bread, mixed green salad, or grilled vegetables.

Overall, risotto is a dish that is beloved by many for its rich, comforting flavor and texture. It's a versatile dish that can be adapted to suit any taste, and it's a great way to showcase the flavors of seasonal ingredients.

History of Risotto

Risotto has been a staple dish in Italian cuisine for centuries, with its origins tracing back to the Northern Italian region of Lombardy, which includes the cities of Milan and Mantua. The dish likely evolved from a popular medieval rice dish called "rice and milk," which was made by cooking rice in milk until it became soft and creamy.

Over time, the recipe for rice and milk evolved to include ingredients like butter, onion, and cheese, eventually becoming the dish we know as risotto today. In the 19th century, the famous Italian chef Pellegrino Artusi published a recipe for risotto in his book "La Scienza in Cucina e l'Arte di Mangiar Bene" (The Science of Cooking and the Art of Eating Well), which helped to popularize the dish outside of Northern Italy.

In addition to its cultural significance, risotto has also played an important role in Italian history. During World War II, rice was a staple food in Northern Italy, and many families survived on dishes like risotto during difficult times.

Today, risotto is enjoyed not only in Italy but all over the world, with variations of the dish being served in restaurants and homes in countless countries. While traditional recipes often include ingredients like Parmesan cheese and butter, many chefs have taken the dish in new and exciting directions, incorporating flavors and ingredients from different cultures and regions.

Despite its evolution over time, however, the basic method of making risotto remains the same, with rice cooked slowly in a broth until it becomes creamy and tender. This technique has been passed down through generations of Italian cooks, and it continues to be a hallmark of the dish today.

Overall, the history of risotto is rich and varied, with the dish evolving over time to become a beloved staple in Italian cuisine and beyond. Its cultural significance and versatility have made it a popular dish all over the world, and it continues to be a favorite of many chefs and home cooks today.

The Basics of Risotto Making

To make a delicious risotto, there are a few key ingredients and techniques that you'll need to master. In this section, we'll cover the essential elements of risotto making, including selecting the right rice, preparing the broth, and cooking the rice to achieve the perfect texture.

1. Selecting the Right Rice

    The most important ingredient in risotto is the rice. Arborio rice is the most commonly used rice for making risotto, but you can also use other varieties such as carnaroli or vialone nano. These types of rice have a high starch content, which is essential for creating the creamy texture that risotto is known for.

2. Preparing the Broth

    The broth is another important element in risotto making. You can use chicken, beef, vegetable, or seafood broth, depending on the recipe you're using. It's important to use a flavorful broth, as this will impart a lot of flavor to the rice. You can make your own broth from scratch or use store-bought broth.

3. Cooking the Rice

To cook risotto, start by sautéing onions or shallots in butter or olive oil until they're softened. Then, add the rice and cook it until it's coated with the butter or oil. Next, add a ladleful of broth to the rice and stir constantly until the liquid is absorbed. Continue adding broth one ladleful at a time, stirring constantly, until the rice is cooked and has a creamy texture.

4. Achieving the Perfect Texture

The key to achieving the perfect texture in risotto is to add the broth slowly, one ladleful at a time, and to stir constantly. This slow and steady process releases the starch from the rice, creating a creamy texture that is characteristic of risotto. It's important not to overcook the rice, as this can result in a mushy texture.

By following these basic steps, you can make a delicious risotto that is rich, creamy, and full of flavor. With practice, you'll become more confident in your risotto making skills and will be able to experiment with different ingredients and flavor combinations to create your own unique versions of this classic Italian dish.

2

Classic Risotto Recipes

Risotto is a versatile dish that can be made with a wide variety of ingredients. In this chapter, we'll explore some classic risotto recipes that have stood the test of time. These recipes are perfect for anyone who is new to risotto making or who simply wants to enjoy the comforting flavors of traditional Italian cuisine.

1. Mushroom Risotto

> Mushroom risotto is a classic dish that is both hearty and comforting. Start by sautéing mushrooms in butter and garlic until they're softened, then add the rice and cook until it's coated with the butter. Add broth one ladleful at a time, stirring constantly, until the rice is cooked and the mushrooms are tender. Finish with Parmesan cheese and chopped parsley.

2. Asparagus Risotto

Asparagus risotto is a light and fresh take on the classic dish. Start by blanching asparagus until it's tender, then chop it into small pieces. Sauté onions in butter or oil, then add the rice and cook until it's coated with the butter. Add broth one ladleful at a time, stirring constantly, until the rice is cooked. Add the chopped asparagus and finish with Parmesan cheese.

3. Saffron Risotto

Saffron risotto is a luxurious dish that is perfect for special occasions. Start by soaking saffron threads in hot broth until the liquid is infused with flavor and color. Sauté onions in butter or oil, then add the rice and cook until it's coated with the butter. Add the saffron-infused broth one ladleful at a time, stirring constantly, until the rice is cooked. Finish with Parmesan cheese.

4. Tomato Risotto

Tomato risotto is a bright and flavorful dish that is perfect for summer. Start by sautéing onions in olive oil, then add diced tomatoes and cook until they're softened. Add the rice and cook until it's coated with the tomato mixture. Add broth one ladleful at a time, stirring constantly, until the rice is cooked. Finish with fresh basil and Parmesan cheese.

5. Pumpkin Risotto

Pumpkin risotto is a warm and comforting dish that is perfect for fall. Start by roasting diced pumpkin until it's tender and caramelized. Sauté onions in butter or oil, then add the rice and cook until it's coated with the butter. Add broth one ladleful at a time, stirring constantly, until the rice is cooked. Add the roasted pumpkin and finish with Parmesan cheese and a sprinkle of nutmeg.

These classic risotto recipes are perfect for anyone who loves traditional Italian cuisine. They're easy to make and can be adapted to suit your own taste preferences. Experiment with different ingredients and flavor combinations to create your own unique risotto dishes.

Recipe: Mushroom Risotto

Ingredients:

- 1 pound mushrooms, sliced (any variety of mushrooms can be used, but shiitake or cremini work well)
- 6 cups chicken or vegetable broth
- 1 small onion, finely chopped
- 2 cloves garlic, minced
- 2 tablespoons butter
- 2 tablespoons olive oil
- 1 1/2 cups arborio rice
- 1/2 cup dry white wine
- 1/2 cup grated Parmesan cheese
- 2 tablespoons chopped fresh parsley
- Salt and pepper to taste

Instructions:

1. In a large pot, heat the broth until it's hot but not boiling. Keep it on low heat throughout the cooking process.
2. In a separate large pot, melt the butter with the olive oil over medium heat. Add the onions and garlic and sauté until they're softened.
3. Add the mushrooms to the pot and sauté for about

5-7 minutes, or until they're tender and have released their liquid.
4. Add the arborio rice to the pot and stir until it's coated with the butter and oil. Cook for about 2-3 minutes, or until the rice is slightly toasted.
5. Pour in the white wine and stir until it's absorbed into the rice.
6. Add one ladleful of hot broth to the pot and stir constantly until the liquid is absorbed. Continue adding broth one ladleful at a time, stirring constantly, until the rice is cooked and has a creamy texture. This should take about 20-25 minutes.
7. When the rice is cooked, remove the pot from the heat and stir in the grated Parmesan cheese and chopped parsley. Season with salt and pepper to taste.
8. Let the risotto sit for a minute or two before serving to allow the flavors to meld together.

Serve the mushroom risotto hot, garnished with additional Parmesan cheese and chopped parsley, if desired. Enjoy!

Recipe: Asparagus Risotto

Ingredients:

- 1 bunch asparagus, trimmed and chopped into small pieces
- 6 cups chicken or vegetable broth
- 1 small onion, finely chopped
- 2 cloves garlic, minced
- 2 tablespoons butter
- 2 tablespoons olive oil
- 1 1/2 cups arborio rice
- 1/2 cup dry white wine
- 1/2 cup grated Parmesan cheese
- 2 tablespoons chopped fresh parsley
- Salt and pepper to taste

Instructions:

1. In a large pot, heat the broth until it's hot but not boiling. Keep it on low heat throughout the cooking process.
2. In a separate large pot, melt the butter with the olive oil over medium heat. Add the onions and garlic and sauté until they're softened.
3. Add the chopped asparagus to the pot and sauté for about 5-7 minutes, or until it's tender.

4. Add the arborio rice to the pot and stir until it's coated with the butter and oil. Cook for about 2-3 minutes, or until the rice is slightly toasted.
5. Pour in the white wine and stir until it's absorbed into the rice.
6. Add one ladleful of hot broth to the pot and stir constantly until the liquid is absorbed. Continue adding broth one ladleful at a time, stirring constantly, until the rice is cooked and has a creamy texture. This should take about 20-25 minutes.
7. When the rice is cooked, remove the pot from the heat and stir in the grated Parmesan cheese and chopped parsley. Season with salt and pepper to taste.
8. Let the risotto sit for a minute or two before serving to allow the flavors to meld together.

Serve the asparagus risotto hot, garnished with additional Parmesan cheese and chopped parsley, if desired. Enjoy!

Recipe: Saffron Risotto

Ingredients:

- 6 cups chicken or vegetable broth
- 1 small onion, finely chopped
- 2 cloves garlic, minced
- 2 tablespoons butter
- 2 tablespoons olive oil
- 1 1/2 cups arborio rice
- 1/2 cup dry white wine
- 1/4 teaspoon saffron threads
- 1/2 cup grated Parmesan cheese
- Salt and pepper to taste

Instructions:

1. In a large pot, heat the broth until it's hot but not boiling. Add the saffron threads to the broth and let it sit for a few minutes to infuse the flavor and color.
2. In a separate large pot, melt the butter with the olive oil over medium heat. Add the onions and garlic and sauté until they're softened.
3. Add the arborio rice to the pot and stir until it's coated with the butter and oil. Cook for about 2-3 minutes, or until the rice is slightly toasted.

4. Pour in the white wine and stir until it's absorbed into the rice.
5. Add one ladleful of hot broth to the pot and stir constantly until the liquid is absorbed. Continue adding broth one ladleful at a time, stirring constantly, until the rice is cooked and has a creamy texture. This should take about 20-25 minutes.
6. When the rice is cooked, remove the pot from the heat and stir in the grated Parmesan cheese. Season with salt and pepper to taste.
7. Let the risotto sit for a minute or two before serving to allow the flavors to meld together.

Serve the saffron risotto hot, garnished with additional Parmesan cheese and a few extra saffron threads, if desired. Enjoy!

Recipe: Tomato Risotto

Ingredients:

- 6 cups chicken or vegetable broth
- 1 small onion, finely chopped
- 2 cloves garlic, minced
- 2 tablespoons olive oil
- 1 1/2 cups arborio rice
- 1/2 cup dry white wine
- 1 can diced tomatoes, drained
- 1/2 cup grated Parmesan cheese
- 2 tablespoons chopped fresh basil
- Salt and pepper to taste

Instructions:

1. In a large pot, heat the broth until it's hot but not boiling. Keep it on low heat throughout the cooking process.
2. In a separate large pot, heat the olive oil over medium heat. Add the onions and garlic and sauté until they're softened.
3. Add the drained diced tomatoes to the pot and cook for 5-7 minutes, or until they're softened and have released their liquid.
4. Add the arborio rice to the pot and stir until it's coated

with the tomato mixture. Cook for about 2-3 minutes, or until the rice is slightly toasted.
5. Pour in the white wine and stir until it's absorbed into the rice.
6. Add one ladleful of hot broth to the pot and stir constantly until the liquid is absorbed. Continue adding broth one ladleful at a time, stirring constantly, until the rice is cooked and has a creamy texture. This should take about 20-25 minutes.
7. When the rice is cooked, remove the pot from the heat and stir in the grated Parmesan cheese and chopped basil. Season with salt and pepper to taste.
8. Let the risotto sit for a minute or two before serving to allow the flavors to meld together.

Serve the tomato risotto hot, garnished with additional Parmesan cheese and chopped basil, if desired. Enjoy!

Recipe: Pumpkin Risotto

Ingredients:

- 1 small pumpkin, peeled, seeded, and diced into small pieces
- 6 cups chicken or vegetable broth
- 1 small onion, finely chopped
- 2 cloves garlic, minced
- 2 tablespoons butter
- 2 tablespoons olive oil
- 1 1/2 cups arborio rice
- 1/2 cup dry white wine
- 1/2 cup grated Parmesan cheese
- 1/4 teaspoon ground nutmeg
- Salt and pepper to taste

Instructions:

1. Preheat the oven to 400°F. Place the diced pumpkin on a baking sheet and roast for 15-20 minutes, or until it's tender and caramelized.
2. In a large pot, heat the broth until it's hot but not boiling. Keep it on low heat throughout the cooking process.
3. In a separate large pot, melt the butter with the olive oil

over medium heat. Add the onions and garlic and sauté until they're softened.
4. Add the arborio rice to the pot and stir until it's coated with the butter and oil. Cook for about 2-3 minutes, or until the rice is slightly toasted.
5. Pour in the white wine and stir until it's absorbed into the rice.
6. Add one ladleful of hot broth to the pot and stir constantly until the liquid is absorbed. Continue adding broth one ladleful at a time, stirring constantly, until the rice is cooked and has a creamy texture. This should take about 20-25 minutes.
7. When the rice is cooked, remove the pot from the heat and stir in the grated Parmesan cheese and roasted pumpkin. Season with salt, pepper, and nutmeg to taste.
8. Let the risotto sit for a minute or two before serving to allow the flavors to meld together.

Serve the pumpkin risotto hot, garnished with additional Parmesan cheese and a sprinkle of nutmeg, if desired. Enjoy!

3

Seafood Risotto Recipes

Risotto is the perfect canvas for showcasing the delicate flavors of seafood. In this chapter, we'll explore some delicious seafood risotto recipes that are perfect for a special occasion or a romantic dinner for two.

1. Shrimp and Pea Risotto

> Shrimp and pea risotto is a classic Italian dish that's both elegant and flavorful. Start by sautéing shrimp in butter until they're pink and cooked through. Remove them from the pan and set them aside. Sauté onions and garlic in the same pan, then add the rice and cook until it's coated with the butter. Add broth one ladleful at a time, stirring constantly, until the rice is cooked. Stir in the cooked shrimp and frozen peas and finish with Parmesan cheese.

2. Scallop Risotto

Scallop risotto is a decadent dish that's perfect for a special occasion. Start by searing scallops in a hot pan until they're golden brown on both sides. Remove them from the pan and set them aside. Sauté onions and garlic in the same pan, then add the rice and cook until it's coated with the butter. Add broth one ladleful at a time, stirring constantly, until the rice is cooked. Stir in the cooked scallops and finish with Parmesan cheese and chopped fresh parsley.

3. Lobster Risotto

Lobster risotto is a luxurious dish that's perfect for a romantic dinner for two. Start by cooking a whole lobster, removing the meat from the shell, and chopping it into small pieces. Sauté onions and garlic in a large pot, then add the rice and cook until it's coated with the butter. Add broth one ladleful at a time, stirring constantly, until the rice is cooked. Stir in the cooked lobster meat and finish with Parmesan cheese.

4. Crab Risotto

Crab risotto is a delicate and flavorful dish that's perfect for showcasing the sweetness of crab meat. Start by sautéing crab meat in butter until it's cooked through. Remove it from the pan and set it aside. Sauté onions and garlic in the same pan, then add the rice and cook until it's coated with the butter. Add broth one ladleful at a time, stirring constantly, until the rice is cooked. Stir in the cooked crab meat and finish with Parmesan cheese and a sprinkle of Old Bay seasoning.

These seafood risotto recipes are perfect for anyone who loves the delicate flavors of seafood. They're easy to make and can be adapted to suit your own taste preferences. Experiment with different seafood and flavor combinations to create your own unique seafood risotto dishes.

Recipe: Shrimp and Pea Risotto

Ingredients:

- 1 pound shrimp, peeled and deveined
- 6 cups chicken or vegetable broth
- 1 small onion, finely chopped
- 2 cloves garlic, minced
- 2 tablespoons butter
- 2 tablespoons olive oil
- 1 1/2 cups arborio rice
- 1/2 cup dry white wine
- 1 cup frozen peas
- 1/2 cup grated Parmesan cheese
- Salt and pepper to taste

Instructions:

1. In a large pot, heat the broth until it's hot but not boiling. Keep it on low heat throughout the cooking process.
2. In a separate large pot, melt the butter with the olive oil over medium heat. Add the onions and garlic and sauté until they're softened.
3. Add the shrimp to the pot and sauté for about 3-4

minutes, or until they're pink and cooked through. Remove the shrimp from the pot and set them aside.
4. Add the arborio rice to the pot and stir until it's coated with the butter and oil. Cook for about 2-3 minutes, or until the rice is slightly toasted.
5. Pour in the white wine and stir until it's absorbed into the rice.
6. Add one ladleful of hot broth to the pot and stir constantly until the liquid is absorbed. Continue adding broth one ladleful at a time, stirring constantly, until the rice is cooked and has a creamy texture. This should take about 20-25 minutes.
7. When the rice is cooked, stir in the cooked shrimp and frozen peas. Cook for another 2-3 minutes, or until the peas are heated through.
8. Remove the pot from the heat and stir in the grated Parmesan cheese. Season with salt and pepper to taste.
9. Let the risotto sit for a minute or two before serving to allow the flavors to meld together.

Serve the shrimp and pea risotto hot, garnished with additional Parmesan cheese and chopped fresh parsley, if desired. Enjoy!

Recipe: Scallop Risotto

Ingredients:

- 1 pound scallops, cleaned
- 6 cups chicken or vegetable broth
- 1 small onion, finely chopped
- 2 cloves garlic, minced
- 2 tablespoons butter
- 2 tablespoons olive oil
- 1 1/2 cups arborio rice
- 1/2 cup dry white wine
- 1/2 cup grated Parmesan cheese
- 2 tablespoons chopped fresh parsley
- Salt and pepper to taste

Instructions:

1. In a large pot, heat the broth until it's hot but not boiling. Keep it on low heat throughout the cooking process.
2. In a separate large pot, heat the olive oil over medium heat. Add the scallops to the pot and cook for about 2-3 minutes on each side, or until they're golden brown and cooked through. Remove the scallops from the pot and set them aside.

3. In the same pot, melt the butter and sauté the onions and garlic until they're softened.
4. Add the arborio rice to the pot and stir until it's coated with the butter and oil. Cook for about 2-3 minutes, or until the rice is slightly toasted.
5. Pour in the white wine and stir until it's absorbed into the rice.
6. Add one ladleful of hot broth to the pot and stir constantly until the liquid is absorbed. Continue adding broth one ladleful at a time, stirring constantly, until the rice is cooked and has a creamy texture. This should take about 20-25 minutes.
7. When the rice is cooked, remove the pot from the heat and stir in the grated Parmesan cheese and chopped parsley. Season with salt and pepper to taste.
8. Let the risotto sit for a minute or two before serving to allow the flavors to meld together.

Serve the scallop risotto hot, garnished with additional Parmesan cheese and a few cooked scallops, if desired. Enjoy!

Recipe: Lobster Risotto

Ingredients:

- 1 whole lobster, cooked and chopped into small pieces
- 6 cups chicken or vegetable broth
- 1 small onion, finely chopped
- 2 cloves garlic, minced
- 2 tablespoons butter
- 2 tablespoons olive oil
- 1 1/2 cups arborio rice
- 1/2 cup dry white wine
- 1/2 cup grated Parmesan cheese
- Salt and pepper to taste

Instructions:

1. In a large pot, heat the broth until it's hot but not boiling. Keep it on low heat throughout the cooking process.
2. In a separate large pot, melt the butter with the olive oil over medium heat. Add the onions and garlic and sauté until they're softened.
3. Add the arborio rice to the pot and stir until it's coated with the butter and oil. Cook for about 2-3 minutes, or until the rice is slightly toasted.

4. Pour in the white wine and stir until it's absorbed into the rice.
5. Add one ladleful of hot broth to the pot and stir constantly until the liquid is absorbed. Continue adding broth one ladleful at a time, stirring constantly, until the rice is cooked and has a creamy texture. This should take about 20-25 minutes.
6. When the rice is cooked, stir in the chopped lobster meat. Cook for another 2-3 minutes, or until the lobster is heated through.
7. Remove the pot from the heat and stir in the grated Parmesan cheese. Season with salt and pepper to taste.
8. Let the risotto sit for a minute or two before serving to allow the flavors to meld together.

Serve the lobster risotto hot, garnished with additional Parmesan cheese and a few pieces of cooked lobster, if desired. Enjoy!

Recipe: Crab Risotto

Ingredients:

- 1 pound lump crab meat
- 6 cups chicken or vegetable broth
- 1 small onion, finely chopped
- 2 cloves garlic, minced
- 2 tablespoons butter
- 2 tablespoons olive oil
- 1 1/2 cups arborio rice
- 1/2 cup dry white wine
- 1/2 cup grated Parmesan cheese
- 1 teaspoon Old Bay seasoning
- Salt and pepper to taste

Instructions:

1. In a large pot, heat the broth until it's hot but not boiling. Keep it on low heat throughout the cooking process.
2. In a separate large pot, melt the butter with the olive oil over medium heat. Add the onions and garlic and sauté until they're softened.
3. Add the crab meat to the pot and sauté for about 2-3 minutes, or until it's cooked through. Remove the crab meat from the pot and set it aside.

4. In the same pot, add the arborio rice and stir until it's coated with the butter and oil. Cook for about 2-3 minutes, or until the rice is slightly toasted.
5. Pour in the white wine and stir until it's absorbed into the rice.
6. Add one ladleful of hot broth to the pot and stir constantly until the liquid is absorbed. Continue adding broth one ladleful at a time, stirring constantly, until the rice is cooked and has a creamy texture. This should take about 20-25 minutes.
7. When the rice is cooked, stir in the cooked crab meat and Old Bay seasoning. Cook for another 2-3 minutes, or until the crab is heated through.
8. Remove the pot from the heat and stir in the grated Parmesan cheese. Season with salt and pepper to taste.
9. Let the risotto sit for a minute or two before serving to allow the flavors to meld together.

Serve the crab risotto hot, garnished with additional Parmesan cheese and a sprinkle of Old Bay seasoning, if desired. Enjoy!

4

Meat Risotto Recipes

In this chapter, we'll explore some delicious meat risotto recipes that are perfect for a hearty and satisfying meal.

1. Chicken Risotto

   Chicken risotto is a comforting and classic dish that's perfect for any occasion. Start by cooking chicken breasts in a separate pan until they're golden brown and cooked through. Remove them from the pan and set them aside. Sauté onions and garlic in a large pot, then add the rice and cook until it's coated with the butter. Add broth one ladleful at a time, stirring constantly, until the rice is cooked. Stir in the cooked chicken and finish with Parmesan cheese.

2. Beef Risotto

Beef risotto is a rich and flavorful dish that's perfect for meat lovers. Start by browning ground beef in a separate pan until it's cooked through. Remove it from the pan and set it aside. Sauté onions and garlic in a large pot, then add the rice and cook until it's coated with the butter. Add broth one ladleful at a time, stirring constantly, until the rice is cooked. Stir in the cooked beef and finish with Parmesan cheese and a sprinkle of fresh thyme.

3. Sausage and Peppers Risotto

Sausage and peppers risotto is a delicious and satisfying dish that's perfect for a cozy night in. Start by cooking Italian sausage in a separate pan until it's browned and cooked through. Remove it from the pan and set it aside. Sauté onions, garlic, and bell peppers in a large pot, then add the rice and cook until it's coated with the butter. Add broth one ladleful at a time, stirring constantly, until the rice is cooked. Stir in the cooked sausage and finish with Parmesan cheese.

4. Pork and Apple Risotto

Pork and apple risotto is a sweet and savory dish that's perfect for fall. Start by cooking diced pork in a separate pan until it's browned and cooked through. Remove it from the pan and set it aside. Sauté onions and garlic in a large pot, then add the rice and cook until it's coated with the butter. Add broth one ladleful at a time, stirring constantly, until the rice is cooked. Stir in the cooked pork, diced apples, and a sprinkle of cinnamon. Finish with Parmesan cheese.

These meat risotto recipes are perfect for anyone who loves a hearty and satisfying meal. They're easy to make and can be adapted to suit your own taste preferences. Experiment with different meats and flavor combinations to create your own unique meat risotto dishes.

Recipe: Chicken Risotto

Ingredients:

- 2 chicken breasts, boneless and skinless
- 6 cups chicken or vegetable broth
- 1 small onion, finely chopped
- 2 cloves garlic, minced
- 2 tablespoons butter
- 2 tablespoons olive oil
- 1 1/2 cups arborio rice
- 1/2 cup dry white wine
- 1/2 cup grated Parmesan cheese
- Salt and pepper to taste

Instructions:

1. In a large pot, heat the broth until it's hot but not boiling. Keep it on low heat throughout the cooking process.
2. In a separate large pan, heat the olive oil over medium heat. Season the chicken breasts with salt and pepper and cook them in the pan for about 5-6 minutes on each side, or until they're golden brown and cooked through. Remove the chicken from the pan and let it cool for a few minutes. Once it's cool enough to handle, chop it into small pieces.

3. In the same pan, melt the butter and sauté the onions and garlic until they're softened.
4. Add the arborio rice to the pan and stir until it's coated with the butter and oil. Cook for about 2-3 minutes, or until the rice is slightly toasted.
5. Pour in the white wine and stir until it's absorbed into the rice.
6. Add one ladleful of hot broth to the pan and stir constantly until the liquid is absorbed. Continue adding broth one ladleful at a time, stirring constantly, until the rice is cooked and has a creamy texture. This should take about 20-25 minutes.
7. When the rice is cooked, stir in the chopped chicken. Cook for another 2-3 minutes, or until the chicken is heated through.
8. Remove the pan from the heat and stir in the grated Parmesan cheese. Season with salt and pepper to taste.
9. Let the risotto sit for a minute or two before serving to allow the flavors to meld together.

Serve the chicken risotto hot, garnished with additional Parmesan cheese and chopped fresh parsley, if desired. Enjoy!

Recipe: Beef Risotto

Ingredients:

- 1 pound ground beef
- 6 cups beef or vegetable broth
- 1 small onion, finely chopped
- 2 cloves garlic, minced
- 2 tablespoons butter
- 2 tablespoons olive oil
- 1 1/2 cups arborio rice
- 1/2 cup dry red wine
- 1/2 cup grated Parmesan cheese
- 1 teaspoon fresh thyme leaves
- Salt and pepper to taste

Instructions:

1. In a large pot, heat the broth until it's hot but not boiling. Keep it on low heat throughout the cooking process.
2. In a separate large pan, brown the ground beef over medium heat, breaking it up with a spatula as it cooks. Once the beef is browned, remove it from the pan and set it aside.
3. In the same pan, melt the butter and sauté the onions and garlic until they're softened.

4. Add the arborio rice to the pan and stir until it's coated with the butter and oil. Cook for about 2-3 minutes, or until the rice is slightly toasted.
5. Pour in the red wine and stir until it's absorbed into the rice.
6. Add one ladleful of hot broth to the pan and stir constantly until the liquid is absorbed. Continue adding broth one ladleful at a time, stirring constantly, until the rice is cooked and has a creamy texture. This should take about 20-25 minutes.
7. When the rice is cooked, stir in the cooked ground beef and thyme leaves. Cook for another 2-3 minutes, or until the beef is heated through.
8. Remove the pan from the heat and stir in the grated Parmesan cheese. Season with salt and pepper to taste.
9. Let the risotto sit for a minute or two before serving to allow the flavors to meld together.

Serve the beef risotto hot, garnished with additional Parmesan cheese and a sprinkle of fresh thyme leaves, if desired. Enjoy!

Recipe: Sausage and Peppers Risotto

Ingredients:

- 1 pound Italian sausage, casing removed and crumbled
- 1 red bell pepper, diced
- 1 green bell pepper, diced
- 1 small onion, finely chopped
- 2 cloves garlic, minced
- 6 cups chicken or vegetable broth
- 2 tablespoons butter
- 2 tablespoons olive oil
- 1 1/2 cups arborio rice
- 1/2 cup dry white wine
- 1/2 cup grated Parmesan cheese
- Salt and pepper to taste

Instructions:

1. In a large pot, heat the broth until it's hot but not boiling. Keep it on low heat throughout the cooking process.
2. In a separate large pan, cook the sausage over medium heat, breaking it up with a spatula as it cooks. Once

the sausage is browned and cooked through, remove it from the pan and set it aside.
3. In the same pan, add the butter and olive oil over medium heat. Sauté the onions and garlic until they're softened.
4. Add the diced bell peppers to the pan and cook for 3-4 minutes, or until they're slightly softened.
5. Add the arborio rice to the pan and stir until it's coated with the butter and oil. Cook for about 2-3 minutes, or until the rice is slightly toasted.
6. Pour in the white wine and stir until it's absorbed into the rice.
7. Add one ladleful of hot broth to the pan and stir constantly until the liquid is absorbed. Continue adding broth one ladleful at a time, stirring constantly, until the rice is cooked and has a creamy texture. This should take about 20-25 minutes.
8. When the rice is cooked, stir in the cooked sausage. Cook for another 2-3 minutes, or until the sausage is heated through.
9. Remove the pan from the heat and stir in the grated Parmesan cheese. Season with salt and pepper to taste.
10. Let the risotto sit for a minute or two before serving to allow the flavors to meld together.

Serve the sausage and peppers risotto hot, garnished with additional Parmesan cheese and a sprinkle of chopped fresh parsley, if desired. Enjoy!

Recipe: Pork and Apple Risotto

Ingredients:

- 1 pound pork tenderloin, trimmed and cut into small pieces
- 2 medium apples, peeled, cored and diced
- 1 small onion, finely chopped
- 2 cloves garlic, minced
- 6 cups chicken or vegetable broth
- 2 tablespoons butter
- 2 tablespoons olive oil
- 1 1/2 cups arborio rice
- 1/2 cup dry white wine
- 1/2 cup grated Parmesan cheese
- 1/2 teaspoon ground cinnamon
- Salt and pepper to taste

Instructions:

1. In a large pot, heat the broth until it's hot but not boiling. Keep it on low heat throughout the cooking process.
2. In a separate large pan, cook the pork over medium heat

until it's browned and cooked through. Once the pork is cooked, remove it from the pan and set it aside.
3. In the same pan, add the butter and olive oil over medium heat. Sauté the onions and garlic until they're softened.
4. Add the diced apples to the pan and cook for 3-4 minutes, or until they're slightly softened.
5. Add the arborio rice to the pan and stir until it's coated with the butter and oil. Cook for about 2-3 minutes, or until the rice is slightly toasted.
6. Pour in the white wine and stir until it's absorbed into the rice.
7. Add one ladleful of hot broth to the pan and stir constantly until the liquid is absorbed. Continue adding broth one ladleful at a time, stirring constantly, until the rice is cooked and has a creamy texture. This should take about 20-25 minutes.
8. When the rice is cooked, stir in the cooked pork and cinnamon. Cook for another 2-3 minutes, or until the pork is heated through.
9. Remove the pan from the heat and stir in the grated Parmesan cheese. Season with salt and pepper to taste.
10. Let the risotto sit for a minute or two before serving to allow the flavors to meld together.

Serve the pork and apple risotto hot, garnished with additional Parmesan cheese and a sprinkle of ground cinnamon, if desired. Enjoy!

5

Vegetable Risotto Recipes

In this chapter, we'll explore some delicious vegetable risotto recipes that are perfect for a meatless meal or as a side dish.

1. Spinach and Feta Risotto

   Spinach and feta risotto is a flavorful and healthy dish that's perfect for any season. Start by sautéing onions and garlic in a large pot, then add the rice and cook until it's coated with the butter. Add broth one ladleful at a time, stirring constantly, until the rice is cooked. Stir in fresh spinach and crumbled feta cheese. Finish with a sprinkle of freshly ground black pepper.

2. Butternut Squash and Sage Risotto

   Butternut squash and sage risotto is a comforting and flavorful dish that's perfect for fall. Start by roasting diced butternut squash in the oven until it's tender and caramelized. Sauté onions and garlic in a large pot, then add the rice and cook until it's coated with the butter. Add broth one ladleful at a time, stirring constantly, until the rice is cooked. Stir in the roasted butternut squash and chopped fresh sage. Finish with Parmesan cheese.

3. Roasted Red Pepper Risotto

Roasted red pepper risotto is a colorful and flavorful dish that's perfect for a vegetarian meal. Start by roasting red bell peppers in the oven until they're tender and slightly charred. Peel and chop the peppers, then sauté them with onions and garlic in a large pot. Add the rice and cook until it's coated with the butter. Add broth one ladleful at a time, stirring constantly, until the rice is cooked. Stir in the roasted red peppers and finish with a sprinkle of chopped fresh parsley.

4. Eggplant and Tomato Risotto

Eggplant and tomato risotto is a delicious and hearty dish that's perfect for a summer meal. Start by roasting diced eggplant in the oven until it's tender and slightly charred. Sauté onions and garlic in a large pot, then add the rice and cook until it's coated with the butter. Add broth one ladleful at a time, stirring constantly, until the rice is cooked. Stir in the roasted eggplant, diced tomatoes, and a sprinkle of chopped fresh basil. Finish with Parmesan cheese.

These vegetable risotto recipes are perfect for anyone who loves a meatless meal or wants to incorporate more vegetables into their diet. They're easy to make and can be adapted to suit your own taste preferences. Experiment with different vegetables and flavor combinations to create your own unique vegetable risotto dishes.

Recipe: Spinach and Feta Risotto

Ingredients:

- 6 cups vegetable or chicken broth
- 1 small onion, finely chopped
- 2 cloves garlic, minced
- 2 tablespoons butter
- 2 tablespoons olive oil
- 1 1/2 cups arborio rice
- 1/2 cup dry white wine
- 2 cups fresh spinach, washed and chopped
- 1/2 cup crumbled feta cheese
- Freshly ground black pepper, to taste

Instructions:

1. In a large pot, heat the broth until it's hot but not boiling. Keep it on low heat throughout the cooking process.
2. In a separate large pan, heat the olive oil over medium heat. Add the onions and garlic and sauté until they're softened.
3. Add the arborio rice to the pan and stir until it's coated

with the butter and oil. Cook for about 2-3 minutes, or until the rice is slightly toasted.
4. Pour in the white wine and stir until it's absorbed into the rice.
5. Add one ladleful of hot broth to the pan and stir constantly until the liquid is absorbed. Continue adding broth one ladleful at a time, stirring constantly, until the rice is cooked and has a creamy texture. This should take about 20-25 minutes.
6. When the rice is cooked, stir in the chopped spinach and crumbled feta cheese. Cook for another 2-3 minutes, or until the spinach is wilted and the feta is heated through.
7. Remove the pan from the heat and season with freshly ground black pepper to taste.
8. Let the risotto sit for a minute or two before serving to allow the flavors to meld together.

Serve the spinach and feta risotto hot, garnished with additional crumbled feta cheese and chopped fresh parsley, if desired. Enjoy!

Recipe: Butternut Squash and Sage Risotto

Ingredients:

- 1 small butternut squash, peeled, seeded and cut into small cubes
- 6 cups vegetable or chicken broth
- 1 small onion, finely chopped
- 2 cloves garlic, minced
- 2 tablespoons butter
- 2 tablespoons olive oil
- 1 1/2 cups arborio rice
- 1/2 cup dry white wine
- 2 tablespoons chopped fresh sage
- 1/2 cup grated Parmesan cheese
- Salt and pepper to taste

Instructions:

1. Preheat your oven to 400°F. Spread the cubed butternut squash on a baking sheet lined with parchment paper. Drizzle with olive oil and sprinkle with salt and pepper. Roast in the oven for about 20-25 minutes or until tender and slightly caramelized.
2. In a large pot, heat the broth until it's hot but not

boiling. Keep it on low heat throughout the cooking process.
3. In a separate large pan, heat the olive oil over medium heat. Add the onions and garlic and sauté until they're softened.
4. Add the arborio rice to the pan and stir until it's coated with the butter and oil. Cook for about 2-3 minutes, or until the rice is slightly toasted.
5. Pour in the white wine and stir until it's absorbed into the rice.
6. Add one ladleful of hot broth to the pan and stir constantly until the liquid is absorbed. Continue adding broth one ladleful at a time, stirring constantly, until the rice is cooked and has a creamy texture. This should take about 20-25 minutes.
7. When the rice is cooked, stir in the roasted butternut squash and chopped sage. Cook for another 2-3 minutes, or until the butternut squash is heated through.
8. Remove the pan from the heat and stir in the grated Parmesan cheese. Season with salt and pepper to taste.
9. Let the risotto sit for a minute or two before serving to allow the flavors to meld together.

Serve the butternut squash and sage risotto hot, garnished with additional grated Parmesan cheese and a sprinkle of chopped fresh sage, if desired. Enjoy!

Recipe: Roasted Red Pepper Risotto

Ingredients:

- 2 red bell peppers, roasted, peeled and chopped
- 6 cups vegetable or chicken broth
- 1 small onion, finely chopped
- 2 cloves garlic, minced
- 2 tablespoons butter
- 2 tablespoons olive oil
- 1 1/2 cups arborio rice
- 1/2 cup dry white wine
- 2 tablespoons chopped fresh parsley
- 1/2 cup grated Parmesan cheese
- Salt and pepper to taste

Instructions:

1. Preheat your oven to 400°F. Place the red bell peppers on a baking sheet lined with parchment paper. Roast in the oven for about 20-25 minutes or until the skin is blistered and blackened.
2. Remove the peppers from the oven and transfer them to a bowl. Cover the bowl with plastic wrap and let the peppers steam for about 10-15 minutes.

3. Once the peppers are cool enough to handle, peel off the skin and remove the seeds. Chop the roasted peppers into small pieces and set aside.
4. In a large pot, heat the broth until it's hot but not boiling. Keep it on low heat throughout the cooking process.
5. In a separate large pan, heat the olive oil over medium heat. Add the onions and garlic and sauté until they're softened.
6. Add the arborio rice to the pan and stir until it's coated with the butter and oil. Cook for about 2-3 minutes, or until the rice is slightly toasted.
7. Pour in the white wine and stir until it's absorbed into the rice.
8. Add one ladleful of hot broth to the pan and stir constantly until the liquid is absorbed. Continue adding broth one ladleful at a time, stirring constantly, until the rice is cooked and has a creamy texture. This should take about 20-25 minutes.
9. When the rice is cooked, stir in the chopped roasted red peppers and chopped parsley. Cook for another 2-3 minutes, or until the peppers are heated through.
10. Remove the pan from the heat and stir in the grated Parmesan cheese. Season with salt and pepper to taste.
11. Let the risotto sit for a minute or two before serving to allow the flavors to meld together.

Serve the roasted red pepper risotto hot, garnished with additional grated Parmesan cheese and a sprinkle of chopped fresh parsley, if desired. Enjoy!

Recipe: Eggplant and Tomato Risotto

Ingredients:

- 1 small eggplant, diced
- 1 cup diced tomatoes
- 6 cups vegetable or chicken broth
- 1 small onion, finely chopped
- 2 cloves garlic, minced
- 2 tablespoons butter
- 2 tablespoons olive oil
- 1 1/2 cups arborio rice
- 1/2 cup dry white wine
- 2 tablespoons chopped fresh basil
- 1/2 cup grated Parmesan cheese
- Salt and pepper to taste

Instructions:

1. Preheat your oven to 400°F. Spread the diced eggplant on a baking sheet lined with parchment paper. Drizzle with olive oil and sprinkle with salt and pepper. Roast in the oven for about 20-25 minutes or until tender and slightly caramelized.
2. In a large pot, heat the broth until it's hot but not

boiling. Keep it on low heat throughout the cooking process.
3. In a separate large pan, heat the olive oil over medium heat. Add the onions and garlic and sauté until they're softened.
4. Add the arborio rice to the pan and stir until it's coated with the butter and oil. Cook for about 2-3 minutes, or until the rice is slightly toasted.
5. Pour in the white wine and stir until it's absorbed into the rice.
6. Add one ladleful of hot broth to the pan and stir constantly until the liquid is absorbed. Continue adding broth one ladleful at a time, stirring constantly, until the rice is cooked and has a creamy texture. This should take about 20-25 minutes.
7. When the rice is cooked, stir in the roasted eggplant, diced tomatoes and chopped fresh basil. Cook for another 2-3 minutes, or until the eggplant is heated through.
8. Remove the pan from the heat and stir in the grated Parmesan cheese. Season with salt and pepper to taste.
9. Let the risotto sit for a minute or two before serving to allow the flavors to meld together.

Serve the eggplant and tomato risotto hot, garnished with additional grated Parmesan cheese and a sprinkle of chopped fresh basil, if desired. Enjoy!

6

Risotto Accompaniments

In this chapter, we'll explore some delicious accompaniments that you can serve with your risotto dishes. These side dishes will complement the flavors of the risotto and make your meal even more satisfying.

1. Garlic Bread

> Garlic bread is a classic accompaniment to risotto. It's easy to make and adds a delicious crunch to your meal. Slice a baguette in half lengthwise and spread a mixture of butter, garlic, and parsley on top. Bake in the oven for 10-15 minutes or until the bread is golden brown and crispy.

2. Mixed Green Salad

> A mixed green salad is a light and refreshing side dish

that pairs perfectly with risotto. Toss together a variety of greens, such as arugula, spinach, and lettuce, with a simple vinaigrette made from olive oil, lemon juice, and Dijon mustard.

3. Grilled Vegetables

Grilled vegetables are a delicious and healthy accompaniment to risotto. Brush sliced vegetables, such as zucchini, eggplant, and bell peppers, with olive oil and grill them until they're tender and slightly charred.

4. Roasted Chicken

Roasted chicken is a hearty and satisfying accompaniment to risotto. Season chicken pieces with salt, pepper, and your favorite herbs, then roast them in the oven until they're golden brown and cooked through. Serve alongside your favorite risotto dish for a complete meal.

These risotto accompaniments are easy to make and will elevate your meal to the next level. Experiment with different side dishes and flavor combinations to find your perfect pairing. Enjoy!

Garlic Bread Recipe

Ingredients:

- 1 baguette
- 1/2 cup unsalted butter, softened
- 3 garlic cloves, minced
- 1 tablespoon chopped fresh parsley
- Salt and pepper to taste

Instructions:

1. Preheat the oven to 375°F.
2. Cut the baguette in half lengthwise and place the halves cut side up on a baking sheet lined with parchment paper.
3. In a small bowl, mix together the softened butter, minced garlic, chopped parsley, salt, and pepper until well combined.
4. Spread the garlic butter mixture over the cut sides of the baguette halves.
5. Bake in the preheated oven for about 10-15 minutes, or until the bread is golden brown and crispy.
6. Remove from the oven and let the garlic bread cool for a few minutes before slicing and serving.

Serve the garlic bread alongside your favorite risotto dish for a delicious and comforting meal. Enjoy!

Mixed Green Salad Recipe

Ingredients:

- 4 cups mixed greens (such as arugula, spinach, and lettuce)
- 1/4 cup extra-virgin olive oil
- 2 tablespoons fresh lemon juice
- 1 teaspoon Dijon mustard
- Salt and pepper to taste

Instructions:

1. Rinse the mixed greens under cold running water and pat them dry with a paper towel. Transfer them to a large salad bowl.
2. In a small bowl, whisk together the olive oil, lemon juice, Dijon mustard, salt, and pepper until well combined.
3. Pour the dressing over the mixed greens and toss to coat evenly.
4. Serve the mixed green salad immediately alongside your favorite risotto dish.

This simple and refreshing salad is the perfect complement to the rich and creamy flavors of risotto. Enjoy!

Grilled Vegetables Recipe

Ingredients:

- 1 zucchini, sliced lengthwise
- 1 eggplant, sliced lengthwise
- 1 red bell pepper, seeded and sliced into strips
- 2 tablespoons extra-virgin olive oil
- Salt and pepper to taste

Instructions:

1. Preheat the grill to medium-high heat.
2. Brush the sliced vegetables with olive oil and sprinkle them with salt and pepper.
3. Place the vegetables on the grill and cook for about 3-5 minutes per side, or until they're tender and slightly charred.
4. Remove the grilled vegetables from the heat and transfer them to a serving platter.
5. Serve the grilled vegetables alongside your favorite risotto dish.

This simple and healthy side dish adds a delicious smoky flavor to your meal. Experiment with different types of vegetables and seasonings to find your perfect combination. Enjoy!

Roasted Chicken Recipe

Ingredients:

- 4 chicken thighs, bone-in and skin-on
- 2 tablespoons extra-virgin olive oil
- 2 cloves garlic, minced
- 1 tablespoon chopped fresh rosemary
- 1 tablespoon chopped fresh thyme
- Salt and pepper to taste

Instructions:

1. Preheat the oven to 375°F.
2. In a small bowl, mix together the olive oil, minced garlic, chopped rosemary, chopped thyme, salt, and pepper until well combined.
3. Place the chicken thighs on a baking sheet lined with parchment paper.
4. Brush the chicken thighs with the olive oil mixture, making sure they're coated evenly.
5. Roast the chicken in the preheated oven for about 35-40 minutes, or until the skin is crispy and the internal temperature reaches 165°F.
6. Remove the chicken from the oven and let it rest for a few minutes before serving.

7. Serve the roasted chicken alongside your favorite risotto dish.

This classic and comforting side dish pairs perfectly with risotto and adds protein and flavor to your meal. Enjoy!

7

Advanced Techniques and Tips

In this chapter, we'll explore some advanced techniques and tips that will take your risotto-making skills to the next level.

1. Stock Preparation

The quality of your stock is crucial to the success of your risotto. To make a rich and flavorful stock, start by simmering chicken or vegetable bones with aromatics, such as onions, carrots, and celery. Skim off any impurities that rise to the surface and let the stock simmer for at least 4 hours, or until it's reduced and concentrated in flavor. Strain the stock and use it as the base for your risotto.

2. Risotto Variations

While classic risotto recipes are always delicious, don't be afraid to experiment with different flavor combinations and ingredients. Try adding saffron, truffle oil, or roasted garlic to your risotto for extra depth of flavor. You can also incorporate different meats, seafood, and vegetables to create unique and delicious variations.

3. Cooking for Large Groups

Risotto can be a great dish to serve at a large gathering or dinner party. To make sure your risotto is ready on time, prepare your stock and ingredients in advance and have them ready to go. When it's time to cook, use a large pot or pan and work in batches to ensure the rice cooks evenly. You can also enlist the help of a friend or family member to stir the risotto while you add the stock.

4. Presentation and Plating Tips

Presentation is key when it comes to risotto. To create a visually appealing dish, use a wide and shallow bowl or plate to serve the risotto. You can also garnish the dish with fresh herbs, grated Parmesan cheese, or a drizzle of olive oil. To achieve a creamy and smooth texture, use a whisk to stir the risotto at the end of the cooking process.

These advanced techniques and tips will help you create delicious and impressive risotto dishes that will impress your friends and family. Experiment with different ingredients and techniques to find your perfect risotto recipe. Enjoy!

Stock Preparation

Ingredients:

- Chicken or vegetable bones
- Aromatics (such as onions, carrots, and celery)
- Water

Instructions:

1. If you're using chicken bones, remove the skin and fat and break the bones into smaller pieces. If you're using vegetable scraps, chop them into small pieces.
2. In a large pot, combine the bones or vegetable scraps with enough water to cover them by a few inches.
3. Add the aromatics, such as roughly chopped onions, carrots, and celery, to the pot.
4. Bring the pot to a boil over high heat, then reduce the heat to low and let the stock simmer for at least 4 hours, or until it's reduced and concentrated in flavor.
5. Skim off any impurities or foam that rise to the surface of the stock using a spoon or a fine-mesh strainer.
6. Once the stock is done, strain it through a fine-mesh strainer into a clean pot or container.
7. Let the stock cool, then store it in the refrigerator for up to 5 days or in the freezer for up to 6 months.

Use this flavorful homemade stock as the base for your risotto for a rich and delicious dish.

Risotto Variations

While classic risotto recipes are always delicious, there are many variations that you can try to create unique and delicious dishes. Here are some ideas to get you started:

1. Mushroom and Parmesan Risotto

    Add sautéed mushrooms and grated Parmesan cheese to your risotto for a rich and savory flavor.

2. Lemon and Shrimp Risotto

    Add lemon juice, lemon zest, and cooked shrimp to your risotto for a fresh and tangy flavor.

3. Tomato and Basil Risotto

    Add canned tomatoes, chopped fresh basil, and grated Parmesan cheese to your risotto for a bright and flavorful dish.

4. Truffle Risotto

    Add truffle oil and grated Parmesan cheese to your risotto for a luxurious and indulgent flavor.

5. Pea and Prosciutto Risotto

   Add cooked peas and diced prosciutto to your risotto for a salty and savory flavor.

6. Asparagus and Lemon Risotto

   Add cooked asparagus and lemon zest to your risotto for a fresh and vibrant flavor.

Experiment with different ingredients and flavor combinations to create your own unique and delicious risotto variations. Enjoy!

Cooking for Large Groups

If you're cooking risotto for a large group, there are a few tips and tricks you can use to ensure that everything goes smoothly. Here are some ideas:

1. Prepare your ingredients in advance

    Before you start cooking, make sure you have all your ingredients measured and chopped and your stock ready to go. This will help you work more efficiently and ensure that everything is ready on time.

2. Use a large pot or pan

    If you're making a large batch of risotto, use a wide and deep pot or pan to ensure that the rice cooks evenly. You don't want to overcrowd the pan, so work in batches if necessary.

3. Enlist help

    If you're cooking for a large group, it can be helpful to have someone else help you stir the risotto while you add the stock. This will help you work more efficiently and ensure that the rice cooks evenly.

4. Serve family-style

   Instead of plating the risotto individually, consider serving it family-style in a large serving dish or bowl. This will make it easier to serve a large group and encourage guests to help themselves.

5. Keep it warm

   Risotto is best served immediately, but if you need to keep it warm for a little while, transfer it to a slow cooker or a large pot set over low heat. Stir it occasionally to prevent the rice from sticking to the bottom.

With these tips and tricks, you can successfully cook risotto for a large group and impress your guests with your culinary skills. Enjoy!

Presentation and Plating Tips

Risotto is a visually appealing dish that can be easily elevated with some simple presentation and plating techniques. Here are some ideas to make your risotto look as good as it tastes:

1. Use a wide, shallow bowl or plate

    Instead of serving risotto in a deep bowl, use a wide, shallow one to showcase the texture and ingredients of the dish.

2. Garnish with fresh herbs

    Sprinkle some chopped fresh herbs, such as parsley, basil, or thyme, over the top of the risotto for a pop of color and flavor.

3. Add texture

    Top the risotto with some toasted nuts or breadcrumbs to add crunch and texture.

4. Create a design

Use a spoon to create a swirl or a design on top of the risotto. This adds a decorative touch and makes the dish look more polished.

5. Use a drizzle or a sauce

Drizzle a little olive oil or a flavored sauce over the top of the risotto to add depth and complexity to the flavors.

6. Use a mold or a ring

Use a mold or a ring to shape the risotto into a perfect circle or square. This is a great way to create a more formal presentation for a special occasion.

By following these tips, you can make your risotto look as good as it tastes and impress your guests with your presentation skills. Enjoy!

8

Conclusion

In this risotto recipe book, we've explored a variety of delicious and flavorful risotto recipes, from classic flavors to seafood, meat, and vegetable variations. We've also covered some advanced techniques and tips to take your risotto-making skills to the next level, including stock preparation, risotto variations, cooking for large groups, and presentation and plating tips.

We hope that this book has inspired you to experiment with different ingredients and techniques to create your own unique and delicious risotto recipes. Remember to always start with high-quality ingredients and take your time when cooking the rice to ensure a creamy and delicious dish.

Final Thoughts:

Risotto is a versatile and comforting dish that can be

enjoyed year-round. It's perfect for a cozy weeknight dinner or a special occasion with friends and family. With a little practice and some experimentation, you can create your own signature risotto recipe that will become a favorite in your household.

Additional Resources:

If you're looking for more inspiration and resources to help you perfect your risotto-making skills, here are some additional resources to check out:

1. Cookbooks: There are many great cookbooks dedicated to risotto recipes and techniques. Check out titles such as "Risotto: Delicious Recipes for Italy's Classic Rice Dish" by Maxine Clark or "The Risotto Cookbook: 25 Creamy and Tasty Risotto Recipes to Perfection" by Gordon Rock.
2. Online resources: There are many websites and blogs dedicated to risotto recipes and techniques. Some of our favorites include Bon Appétit, Epicurious, and Serious Eats.
3. Cooking classes: If you're looking for a more hands-on learning experience, consider taking a cooking class or workshop focused on risotto. Many culinary schools and cooking schools offer classes on Italian cuisine and risotto-making.

We hope you enjoyed this risotto recipe book and found it helpful in your culinary adventures. Happy cooking!

9

Bonus Recipes

Bonus Recipe 1: Mushroom and Parmesan Risotto

Ingredients:

- 6 cups of chicken or vegetable stock
- 2 tablespoons of unsalted butter
- 1 tablespoon of olive oil
- 1 medium onion, finely chopped
- 2 garlic cloves, minced
- 2 cups of Arborio rice
- 1/2 cup of dry white wine
- 8 ounces of mushrooms, sliced
- 1/2 cup of grated Parmesan cheese
- Salt and black pepper, to taste
- Fresh parsley or thyme, chopped for garnish (optional)

Instructions:

1. In a medium pot, bring the chicken or vegetable stock to a simmer over low heat. Keep it warm.
2. In a large, heavy-bottomed pot or Dutch oven, heat the butter and olive oil over medium heat until the butter is melted.
3. Add the onion and garlic to the pot and sauté until the onion is translucent, about 5 minutes.

4. Add the Arborio rice to the pot and stir to coat it with the butter and olive oil. Toast the rice for about 2 minutes, stirring frequently.
5. Add the white wine to the pot and stir until it's absorbed by the rice.
6. Add a ladleful of warm stock to the pot and stir the rice constantly until the stock is absorbed. Repeat this process, adding one ladleful of stock at a time, stirring constantly and letting each addition of stock be absorbed before adding the next.
7. While the risotto is cooking, sauté the mushrooms in a separate pan until they are browned and tender.
8. When the rice is al dente (tender but still firm to the bite), stir in the sautéed mushrooms and grated Parmesan cheese.
9. Season the risotto with salt and black pepper to taste.
10. Serve the mushroom and Parmesan risotto hot, garnished with fresh parsley or thyme if desired.

Enjoy your delicious and savory mushroom and Parmesan risotto!

Bonus Recipe 2: Lemon and Shrimp Risotto

Ingredients:

- 6 cups of chicken or vegetable stock
- 2 tablespoons of unsalted butter
- 1 tablespoon of olive oil
- 1 medium onion, finely chopped
- 2 garlic cloves, minced
- 2 cups of Arborio rice
- 1/2 cup of dry white wine
- 1 pound of medium-sized shrimp, peeled and deveined
- 1/4 cup of fresh lemon juice
- 2 teaspoons of lemon zest
- Salt and black pepper, to taste
- Fresh parsley, chopped for garnish (optional)

Instructions:

1. In a medium pot, bring the chicken or vegetable stock to a simmer over low heat. Keep it warm.
2. In a large, heavy-bottomed pot or Dutch oven, heat the butter and olive oil over medium heat until the butter is melted.

3. Add the onion and garlic to the pot and sauté until the onion is translucent, about 5 minutes.
4. Add the Arborio rice to the pot and stir to coat it with the butter and olive oil. Toast the rice for about 2 minutes, stirring frequently.
5. Add the white wine to the pot and stir until it's absorbed by the rice.
6. Add a ladleful of warm stock to the pot and stir the rice constantly until the stock is absorbed. Repeat this process, adding one ladleful of stock at a time, stirring constantly and letting each addition of stock be absorbed before adding the next.
7. While the risotto is cooking, cook the shrimp in a separate pan until they are pink and cooked through.
8. When the rice is al dente (tender but still firm to the bite), stir in the cooked shrimp, lemon juice, and lemon zest.
9. Season the risotto with salt and black pepper to taste.
10. Serve the lemon and shrimp risotto hot, garnished with fresh parsley if desired.

Enjoy your fresh and tangy lemon and shrimp risotto!

Bonus Recipe 3: Tomato and Basil Risotto

Ingredients:

- 6 cups of chicken or vegetable stock
- 2 tablespoons of unsalted butter
- 1 tablespoon of olive oil
- 1 medium onion, finely chopped
- 2 garlic cloves, minced
- 2 cups of Arborio rice
- 1/2 cup of dry white wine
- 1 can of diced tomatoes (14.5 ounces)
- 1/4 cup of fresh basil, chopped
- 1/2 cup of grated Parmesan cheese
- Salt and black pepper, to taste

Instructions:

1. In a medium pot, bring the chicken or vegetable stock to a simmer over low heat. Keep it warm.
2. In a large, heavy-bottomed pot or Dutch oven, heat the butter and olive oil over medium heat until the butter is melted.
3. Add the onion and garlic to the pot and sauté until the onion is translucent, about 5 minutes.

4. Add the Arborio rice to the pot and stir to coat it with the butter and olive oil. Toast the rice for about 2 minutes, stirring frequently.
5. Add the white wine to the pot and stir until it's absorbed by the rice.
6. Add a ladleful of warm stock to the pot and stir the rice constantly until the stock is absorbed. Repeat this process, adding one ladleful of stock at a time, stirring constantly and letting each addition of stock be absorbed before adding the next.
7. While the risotto is cooking, drain the canned tomatoes and reserve the juice. Add the drained tomatoes to the risotto and stir to combine.
8. Add the reserved tomato juice to the pot and continue cooking the risotto until the rice is al dente (tender but still firm to the bite).
9. Stir in the chopped fresh basil and grated Parmesan cheese.
10. Season the risotto with salt and black pepper to taste.
11. Serve the tomato and basil risotto hot, garnished with additional chopped basil and Parmesan cheese if desired.

Enjoy your bright and flavorful tomato and basil risotto!

Bonus Recipe 4: Truffle Risotto

Ingredients:

- 6 cups of chicken or vegetable stock
- 2 tablespoons of unsalted butter
- 1 tablespoon of olive oil
- 1 medium onion, finely chopped
- 2 garlic cloves, minced
- 2 cups of Arborio rice
- 1/2 cup of dry white wine
- 2 tablespoons of truffle oil
- 1/2 cup of grated Parmesan cheese
- Salt and black pepper, to taste
- Fresh parsley or thyme, chopped for garnish (optional)

Instructions:

1. In a medium pot, bring the chicken or vegetable stock to a simmer over low heat. Keep it warm.
2. In a large, heavy-bottomed pot or Dutch oven, heat the butter and olive oil over medium heat until the butter is melted.
3. Add the onion and garlic to the pot and sauté until the onion is translucent, about 5 minutes.

4. Add the Arborio rice to the pot and stir to coat it with the butter and olive oil. Toast the rice for about 2 minutes, stirring frequently.
5. Add the white wine to the pot and stir until it's absorbed by the rice.
6. Add a ladleful of warm stock to the pot and stir the rice constantly until the stock is absorbed. Repeat this process, adding one ladleful of stock at a time, stirring constantly and letting each addition of stock be absorbed before adding the next.
7. While the risotto is cooking, add the truffle oil to the pot and stir to combine.
8. Continue cooking the risotto until the rice is al dente (tender but still firm to the bite).
9. Stir in the grated Parmesan cheese.
10. Season the risotto with salt and black pepper to taste.
11. Serve the truffle risotto hot, garnished with fresh parsley or thyme if desired.

Enjoy your luxurious and indulgent truffle risotto!

Creative Recipe 1: Risotto with butternut squash, goat cheese, and crispy sage

Ingredients:

- 6 cups of chicken or vegetable stock
- 2 tablespoons of unsalted butter
- 1 tablespoon of olive oil
- 1 medium onion, finely chopped
- 2 garlic cloves, minced
- 2 cups of Arborio rice
- 1/2 cup of dry white wine
- 2 cups of butternut squash, peeled and diced
- 4 ounces of goat cheese, crumbled
- 1/4 cup of fresh sage leaves
- Salt and black pepper, to taste
- Fresh thyme, chopped for garnish (optional)

Instructions:

1. In a medium pot, bring the chicken or vegetable stock to a simmer over low heat. Keep it warm.
2. In a large, heavy-bottomed pot or Dutch oven, heat the butter and olive oil over medium heat until the butter is melted.

3. Add the onion and garlic to the pot and sauté until the onion is translucent, about 5 minutes.
4. Add the Arborio rice to the pot and stir to coat it with the butter and olive oil. Toast the rice for about 2 minutes, stirring frequently.
5. Add the white wine to the pot and stir until it's absorbed by the rice.
6. Add a ladleful of warm stock to the pot and stir the rice constantly until the stock is absorbed. Repeat this process, adding one ladleful of stock at a time, stirring constantly and letting each addition of stock be absorbed before adding the next.
7. While the risotto is cooking, roast the butternut squash in the oven at 400°F for 20-25 minutes, until it's tender and lightly browned.
8. In a separate pan, fry the sage leaves in a little bit of olive oil until they are crispy. Remove them from the pan and place them on a paper towel to drain.
9. When the rice is al dente (tender but still firm to the bite), stir in the roasted butternut squash and crumbled goat cheese.
10. Season the risotto with salt and black pepper to taste.
11. Serve the butternut squash and goat cheese risotto hot, garnished with the crispy sage leaves and fresh thyme if desired.

Enjoy your delicious and unique butternut squash, goat cheese, and crispy sage risotto!

Creative Recipe 2: Risotto with wild mushrooms, caramelized onions, and a splash of white truffle oil

Ingredients:

- 6 cups of chicken or vegetable stock
- 2 tablespoons of unsalted butter
- 1 tablespoon of olive oil
- 1 large onion, thinly sliced
- 2 garlic cloves, minced
- 2 cups of Arborio rice
- 1/2 cup of dry white wine
- 2 cups of wild mushrooms, sliced
- 1/4 cup of heavy cream
- 1 tablespoon of white truffle oil
- 1/2 cup of grated Parmesan cheese
- Salt and black pepper, to taste
- Fresh parsley or thyme, chopped for garnish (optional)

Instructions:

1. In a medium pot, bring the chicken or vegetable stock to a simmer over low heat. Keep it warm.

2. In a large, heavy-bottomed pot or Dutch oven, heat the butter and olive oil over medium heat until the butter is melted.
3. Add the sliced onion to the pot and cook over medium-low heat, stirring occasionally, until the onion is caramelized and golden brown, about 20-25 minutes.
4. Add the minced garlic to the pot and sauté for another minute.
5. Add the Arborio rice to the pot and stir to coat it with the butter and olive oil. Toast the rice for about 2 minutes, stirring frequently.
6. Add the white wine to the pot and stir until it's absorbed by the rice.
7. Add a ladleful of warm stock to the pot and stir the rice constantly until the stock is absorbed. Repeat this process, adding one ladleful of stock at a time, stirring constantly and letting each addition of stock be absorbed before adding the next.
8. While the risotto is cooking, sauté the wild mushrooms in a separate pan until they are tender and lightly browned.
9. When the rice is al dente (tender but still firm to the bite), stir in the caramelized onions, sautéed mushrooms, heavy cream, white truffle oil, and grated Parmesan cheese.
10. Season the risotto with salt and black pepper to taste.
11. Serve the wild mushroom and caramelized onion risotto hot, garnished with fresh parsley or thyme if desired.

Enjoy your creamy and flavorful wild mushroom and caramelized onion risotto!

Creative Recipe 3: Risotto with fresh peas, lemon, and mint

Ingredients:

- 6 cups of chicken or vegetable stock
- 2 tablespoons of unsalted butter
- 1 tablespoon of olive oil
- 1 medium onion, finely chopped
- 2 garlic cloves, minced
- 2 cups of Arborio rice
- 1/2 cup of dry white wine
- 2 cups of fresh peas, shelled
- 1 lemon, zest and juice
- 1/4 cup of fresh mint leaves, chopped
- 1/2 cup of grated Parmesan cheese
- Salt and black pepper, to taste

Instructions:

1. In a medium pot, bring the chicken or vegetable stock to a simmer over low heat. Keep it warm.
2. In a large, heavy-bottomed pot or Dutch oven, heat the butter and olive oil over medium heat until the butter is melted.

3. Add the onion and garlic to the pot and sauté until the onion is translucent, about 5 minutes.
4. Add the Arborio rice to the pot and stir to coat it with the butter and olive oil. Toast the rice for about 2 minutes, stirring frequently.
5. Add the white wine to the pot and stir until it's absorbed by the rice.
6. Add a ladleful of warm stock to the pot and stir the rice constantly until the stock is absorbed. Repeat this process, adding one ladleful of stock at a time, stirring constantly and letting each addition of stock be absorbed before adding the next.
7. While the risotto is cooking, blanch the fresh peas in a separate pot of boiling salted water for about 2-3 minutes, until they are tender but still slightly crisp. Drain and set aside.
8. When the rice is al dente (tender but still firm to the bite), stir in the blanched peas, lemon zest and juice, chopped mint leaves, and grated Parmesan cheese.
9. Season the risotto with salt and black pepper to taste.
10. Serve the fresh pea, lemon, and mint risotto hot, garnished with additional chopped mint leaves and grated Parmesan cheese if desired.

Enjoy your vibrant and refreshing fresh pea, lemon, and mint risotto!

Creative Recipe 4: Risotto with sausage, kale, and Parmesan cheese

Ingredients:

- 6 cups of chicken or vegetable stock
- 2 tablespoons of unsalted butter
- 1 tablespoon of olive oil
- 1 medium onion, finely chopped
- 2 garlic cloves, minced
- 2 cups of Arborio rice
- 1/2 cup of dry white wine
- 1 pound of Italian sausage, casings removed and crumbled
- 2 cups of kale, chopped
- 1/2 cup of grated Parmesan cheese
- Salt and black pepper, to taste

Instructions:

1. In a medium pot, bring the chicken or vegetable stock to a simmer over low heat. Keep it warm.
2. In a large, heavy-bottomed pot or Dutch oven, heat the butter and olive oil over medium heat until the butter is melted.

3. Add the onion and garlic to the pot and sauté until the onion is translucent, about 5 minutes.
4. Add the Arborio rice to the pot and stir to coat it with the butter and olive oil. Toast the rice for about 2 minutes, stirring frequently.
5. Add the white wine to the pot and stir until it's absorbed by the rice.
6. Add a ladleful of warm stock to the pot and stir the rice constantly until the stock is absorbed. Repeat this process, adding one ladleful of stock at a time, stirring constantly and letting each addition of stock be absorbed before adding the next.
7. While the risotto is cooking, brown the Italian sausage in a separate pan over medium-high heat until it's cooked through and lightly browned.
8. Add the chopped kale to the pan with the sausage and sauté until the kale is wilted and tender.
9. When the rice is al dente (tender but still firm to the bite), stir in the cooked sausage and kale, and grated Parmesan cheese.
10. Season the risotto with salt and black pepper to taste.
11. Serve the sausage, kale, and Parmesan risotto hot, garnished with additional grated Parmesan cheese and black pepper if desired.

Enjoy your hearty and comforting sausage, kale, and Parmesan risotto!

Creative Recipe 5: Risotto with lobster, saffron, and brandy

Ingredients:

- 6 cups of chicken or seafood stock
- 2 tablespoons of unsalted butter
- 1 tablespoon of olive oil
- 1 medium onion, finely chopped
- 2 garlic cloves, minced
- 2 cups of Arborio rice
- 1/2 cup of dry white wine
- 1/2 cup of brandy
- 1/2 teaspoon of saffron threads
- 2 lobster tails, cooked and chopped
- 1/2 cup of heavy cream
- 1/2 cup of grated Parmesan cheese
- Salt and black pepper, to taste
- Fresh parsley or chives, chopped for garnish (optional)

Instructions:

1. In a medium pot, bring the chicken or seafood stock to a simmer over low heat. Keep it warm.
2. In a large, heavy-bottomed pot or Dutch oven, heat the

butter and olive oil over medium heat until the butter is melted.
3. Add the onion and garlic to the pot and sauté until the onion is translucent, about 5 minutes.
4. Add the Arborio rice to the pot and stir to coat it with the butter and olive oil. Toast the rice for about 2 minutes, stirring frequently.
5. Add the white wine to the pot and stir until it's absorbed by the rice.
6. Add a ladleful of warm stock to the pot and stir the rice constantly until the stock is absorbed. Repeat this process, adding one ladleful of stock at a time, stirring constantly and letting each addition of stock be absorbed before adding the next.
7. While the risotto is cooking, combine the brandy and saffron threads in a small bowl and set aside.
8. When the rice is almost al dente (tender but still firm to the bite), stir in the cooked lobster, brandy-saffron mixture, heavy cream, and grated Parmesan cheese.
9. Continue cooking the risotto, adding more stock as needed and stirring constantly, until the rice is al dente and the sauce is creamy and thick.
10. Season the risotto with salt and black pepper to taste.
11. Serve the lobster, saffron, and brandy risotto hot, garnished with fresh parsley or chives if desired.

Enjoy your rich and decadent lobster, saffron, and brandy risotto!

Vegan Recipe 1: Vegan risotto with roasted butternut squash, sage, and cashew cream

Ingredients:

- 6 cups of vegetable stock
- 2 tablespoons of olive oil
- 1 medium onion, finely chopped
- 2 garlic cloves, minced
- 2 cups of Arborio rice
- 1/2 cup of dry white wine
- 2 cups of roasted butternut squash, mashed or diced
- 1/4 cup of chopped fresh sage
- 1/2 cup of cashew cream*
- Salt and black pepper, to taste

*To make cashew cream, soak 1 cup of raw cashews in water for at least 4 hours or overnight. Drain the cashews and blend them in a blender or food processor with 1/2 cup of water until smooth and creamy.

Instructions:

1. In a medium pot, bring the vegetable stock to a simmer over low heat. Keep it warm.
2. In a large, heavy-bottomed pot or Dutch oven, heat the olive oil over medium heat.
3. Add the onion and garlic to the pot and sauté until the onion is translucent, about 5 minutes.
4. Add the Arborio rice to the pot and stir to coat it with the olive oil. Toast the rice for about 2 minutes, stirring frequently.
5. Add the white wine to the pot and stir until it's absorbed by the rice.
6. Add a ladleful of warm stock to the pot and stir the rice constantly until the stock is absorbed. Repeat this process, adding one ladleful of stock at a time, stirring constantly and letting each addition of stock be absorbed before adding the next.
7. While the risotto is cooking, roast the butternut squash in a preheated oven at 400°F for about 25-30 minutes, or until it's tender and lightly browned. Mash or dice the roasted squash and set aside.
8. When the rice is almost al dente (tender but still firm to the bite), stir in the roasted butternut squash, chopped sage, and cashew cream.
9. Continue cooking the risotto, adding more stock as needed and stirring constantly, until the rice is al dente and the sauce is creamy and thick.
10. Season the risotto with salt and black pepper to taste.
11. Serve the butternut squash, sage, and cashew cream risotto hot, garnished with additional chopped sage if desired.

Enjoy your creamy and flavorful vegan risotto with roasted butternut squash, sage, and cashew cream!

Vegan Recipe 2: Vegan risotto with roasted beetroot, walnuts, and vegan goat cheese

Ingredients:

- 6 cups of vegetable stock
- 2 tablespoons of olive oil
- 1 medium onion, finely chopped
- 2 garlic cloves, minced
- 2 cups of Arborio rice
- 1/2 cup of dry white wine
- 2 cups of roasted beetroot, diced
- 1/2 cup of chopped walnuts
- 1/2 cup of vegan goat cheese, crumbled
- Salt and black pepper, to taste
- Fresh parsley, chopped for garnish (optional)

Instructions:

1. In a medium pot, bring the vegetable stock to a simmer over low heat. Keep it warm.
2. In a large, heavy-bottomed pot or Dutch oven, heat the olive oil over medium heat.

3. Add the onion and garlic to the pot and sauté until the onion is translucent, about 5 minutes.
4. Add the Arborio rice to the pot and stir to coat it with the olive oil. Toast the rice for about 2 minutes, stirring frequently.
5. Add the white wine to the pot and stir until it's absorbed by the rice.
6. Add a ladleful of warm stock to the pot and stir the rice constantly until the stock is absorbed. Repeat this process, adding one ladleful of stock at a time, stirring constantly and letting each addition of stock be absorbed before adding the next.
7. While the risotto is cooking, roast the beetroot in a preheated oven at 400°F for about 25-30 minutes, or until it's tender and lightly browned. Dice the roasted beetroot and set aside.
8. Toast the chopped walnuts in a separate pan over medium heat until they're lightly browned and fragrant.
9. When the rice is almost al dente (tender but still firm to the bite), stir in the roasted beetroot, chopped walnuts, and crumbled vegan goat cheese.
10. Continue cooking the risotto, adding more stock as needed and stirring constantly, until the rice is al dente and the sauce is creamy and thick.
11. Season the risotto with salt and black pepper to taste.
12. Serve the beetroot, walnut, and vegan goat cheese risotto hot, garnished with fresh parsley if desired.

Enjoy your delicious and colorful vegan risotto with roasted beetroot, walnuts, and vegan goat cheese!

Vegan Recipe 3: Vegan risotto with wild mushrooms, thyme, and cashew cream

Ingredients:

- 6 cups of vegetable stock
- 2 tablespoons of olive oil
- 1 medium onion, finely chopped
- 2 garlic cloves, minced
- 2 cups of Arborio rice
- 1/2 cup of dry white wine
- 2 cups of mixed wild mushrooms, sliced
- 1/4 cup of chopped fresh thyme
- 1/2 cup of cashew cream*
- Salt and black pepper, to taste

*To make cashew cream, soak 1 cup of raw cashews in water for at least 4 hours or overnight. Drain the cashews and blend them in a blender or food processor with 1/2 cup of water until smooth and creamy.

Instructions:

1. In a medium pot, bring the vegetable stock to a simmer over low heat. Keep it warm.
2. In a large, heavy-bottomed pot or Dutch oven, heat the olive oil over medium heat.
3. Add the onion and garlic to the pot and sauté until the onion is translucent, about 5 minutes.
4. Add the Arborio rice to the pot and stir to coat it with the olive oil. Toast the rice for about 2 minutes, stirring frequently.
5. Add the white wine to the pot and stir until it's absorbed by the rice.
6. Add a ladleful of warm stock to the pot and stir the rice constantly until the stock is absorbed. Repeat this process, adding one ladleful of stock at a time, stirring constantly and letting each addition of stock be absorbed before adding the next.
7. While the risotto is cooking, sauté the mixed wild mushrooms in a separate pan over medium heat until they're tender and lightly browned. Set aside.
8. When the rice is almost al dente (tender but still firm to the bite), stir in the sautéed mushrooms, chopped thyme, and cashew cream.
9. Continue cooking the risotto, adding more stock as needed and stirring constantly, until the rice is al dente and the sauce is creamy and thick.
10. Season the risotto with salt and black pepper to taste.
11. Serve the wild mushroom, thyme, and cashew cream risotto hot, garnished with additional chopped thyme if desired.

Enjoy your creamy and comforting vegan risotto with wild mushrooms, thyme, and cashew cream!

Vegan Recipe 4: Vegan risotto with roasted Brussels sprouts, garlic, and vegan sausage

Ingredients:

- 6 cups of vegetable stock
- 2 tablespoons of olive oil
- 1 medium onion, finely chopped
- 2 garlic cloves, minced
- 2 cups of Arborio rice
- 1/2 cup of dry white wine
- 2 cups of roasted Brussels sprouts, halved or quartered
- 4 cloves of garlic, minced
- 1/2 cup of crumbled vegan sausage
- Salt and black pepper, to taste
- Fresh parsley, chopped for garnish (optional)

Instructions:

1. In a medium pot, bring the vegetable stock to a simmer over low heat. Keep it warm.
2. In a large, heavy-bottomed pot or Dutch oven, heat the olive oil over medium heat.

3. Add the onion and garlic to the pot and sauté until the onion is translucent, about 5 minutes.
4. Add the Arborio rice to the pot and stir to coat it with the olive oil. Toast the rice for about 2 minutes, stirring frequently.
5. Add the white wine to the pot and stir until it's absorbed by the rice.
6. Add a ladleful of warm stock to the pot and stir the rice constantly until the stock is absorbed. Repeat this process, adding one ladleful of stock at a time, stirring constantly and letting each addition of stock be absorbed before adding the next.
7. While the risotto is cooking, roast the Brussels sprouts in a preheated oven at 400°F for about 25-30 minutes, or until they're tender and lightly browned. Mince the roasted garlic and set aside.
8. Crumble the vegan sausage and sauté it in a separate pan over medium heat until it's lightly browned and crispy. Set aside.
9. When the rice is almost al dente (tender but still firm to the bite), stir in the roasted Brussels sprouts, minced garlic, and crumbled vegan sausage.
10. Continue cooking the risotto, adding more stock as needed and stirring constantly, until the rice is al dente and the sauce is creamy and thick.
11. Season the risotto with salt and black pepper to taste.
12. Serve the Brussels sprouts, garlic, and vegan sausage risotto hot, garnished with fresh parsley if desired.

Enjoy your savory and hearty vegan risotto with roasted Brussels sprouts, garlic, and vegan sausage!

Epilogue

Thank you for taking the time to explore this collection of risotto recipes. We hope that you've enjoyed cooking and experimenting with the different flavors and ingredients in these recipes. Risotto is a versatile and comforting dish that can be customized to your personal taste and preferences. With the right technique and ingredients, you can create a rich and creamy risotto that will satisfy any craving. Remember to have fun and don't be afraid to try new variations and combinations. We wish you all the best on your culinary adventures, and may your risotto always be delicious!

Glossary of Terms

Here's a glossary of some common terms used in risotto making:

1. Arborio rice: A short-grain Italian rice that is high in starch and commonly used in risotto.
2. Broth/Stock: A liquid made by simmering meat, vegetables, and/or herbs in water, used as the base for many risotto recipes.
3. Carnaroli rice: Another short-grain Italian rice that is often used in risotto making for its high starch content and ability to maintain its texture during cooking.
4. Mantecatura: The final step in risotto making where butter and grated cheese are added to the cooked rice to make the dish creamy and smooth.
5. Soffritto: A mixture of finely chopped onion, celery, and carrot that is sautéed in oil or butter at the beginning of many Italian dishes, including risotto.
6. Toasting: The process of sautéing rice in oil or butter before adding liquid to release its nutty aroma and enhance its flavor.
7. Veggie broth/stock: A vegetarian or vegan version of broth/stock made with vegetables, herbs, and water.
8. Bianco risotto: A basic risotto made without any additional ingredients other than the basic broth, butter, and Parmesan cheese.

9. Brodo: A traditional Italian meat-based broth used in risotto making.
10. Mantecare: The act of stirring vigorously at the end of cooking to incorporate the butter and cheese and create a creamy texture in the risotto.

ALSO BY THE AUTHOR

Also by Edwin Beltran

Business
Pursuing Entrepreneurship: Turning Your Passion into a Business

Recipe
Creamy Delights: A Collection of Cream-based Pasta Recipes
Pasta without Tomatoes or Cream: Delicious and Creative Recipes for Pasta Lovers
Pasta!
The Complete Guide to Risotto: Delicious Recipes and Expert Techniques
Tomato-Based Pasta: Delicious Recipes for Every Occasion

Self Help
Career Development – Tips for finding purpose, advancing in a career, and achieving success
Health and Wellness
Leadership and Management
Mastering Emotional Intelligence: A Self-Help Guide
Mindfulness and Meditation
Motivation and Inspiration
Personal Growth and Development
Relationships
Self-Confidence and Self-Esteem
Time Management and Productivity

CPSIA information can be obtained
at www.ICGtesting.com
Printed in the USA
BVHW080758140623
665881BV00014B/688